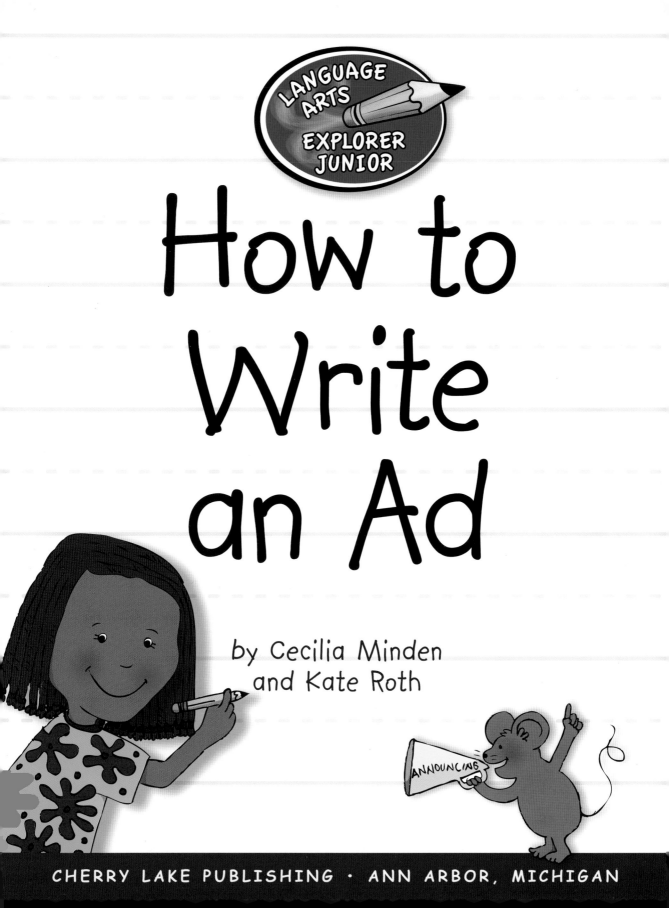

LANGUAGE ARTS EXPLORER JUNIOR

How to Write an Ad

by Cecilia Minden
and Kate Roth

ANNOUNCING

CHERRY LAKE PUBLISHING · ANN ARBOR, MICHIGAN

Published in the United States of America by Cherry Lake Publishing
Ann Arbor, Michigan
www.cherrylakepublishing.com

Content Adviser: Jeannette Mancilla-Martinez, EdD, Assistant Professor of
Literacy, Language, and Culture, University of Illinois at Chicago

Design and Illustration: The Design Lab

Photo Credits: Page 5, ©Patrick Batchelder/Alamy; page 6, ©archana
bhartia/Shutterstock, Inc.; page 15, ©gsmad/Shutterstock, Inc.; page 17,
©Media Bakery; page 21, ©David R. Frazier, Photolibrary, Inc./Alamy

Library of Congress Cataloging-in-Publication Data
Minden, Cecilia.
  How to write an ad/by Cecilia Minden and Kate Roth.
     p. cm.—(Language Arts explorer junior)
  Includes bibliographical references and index.
  ISBN-13: 978-1-61080-107-2 (lib. bdg.)
  ISBN-13: 978-1-61080-279-6 (pbk.)
  1. Advertising—Juvenile literature. I. Roth, Kate. II. Title. III. Series.
  HF5829.M56 2011
  659.1—dc22   2010053594

Cherry Lake Publishing would like to acknowledge the work
of The Partnership for 21st Century Skills. Please visit
www.21stcenturyskills.org for more information.

Printed in the United States of America
Corporate Graphics Inc.
July 2011
CLFA09

Table of Contents

CHAPTER ONE

Be Persuasive! 4

CHAPTER TWO

The Way Ads Work 6

CHAPTER THREE

Your Attention Please! 10

CHAPTER FOUR

Made You Look! 14

CHAPTER FIVE

Bringing Everything Together. . .17

CHAPTER SIX

Final Check 20

Glossary 22

For More Information 23

Index 24

About the Authors 24

Be Persuasive!

Have you ever talked your grandma into getting you a toy? Maybe you talked your best friend into joining a team. These are both examples of you being **persuasive**.

Are you good at persuading people to do things you want them to do?

You see **advertisements** every day. We call them "ads" for short. Ads try to persuade you to do something.

Ads can be found almost anywhere you look.

CHAPTER TWO

The Way Ads Work

Pay close attention to the ads the next time you read a newspaper.

Look through magazines and newspapers. Which ads get your **attention**? Reading ads is a good way to learn how to write them. Sales ads try to persuade people to buy things.

Other ads are not about sales. They are more like **announcements**. These ads tell people about upcoming events. Most ads try to answer four questions:

1. *What* is for sale? or *What* is happening?
2. *Why* should someone buy what is being sold? or *Why* should someone go to this event?
3. *Where* can someone buy what is being sold? or *Where* is this event happening?
4. *When* can someone buy what is being sold, and how long will the sale last? or *When* is this event happening?

Ads often list other information too. For example, a sales ad might include prices. An ad for a contest probably explains the contest's rules.

Most ads use persuasive words. Many include action words. "Come," "see," and "listen" are words that tell us to take action. Other phrases or groups of words have special meanings that also make them persuasive. A few examples are "new and improved," "this week only," and "experts agree."

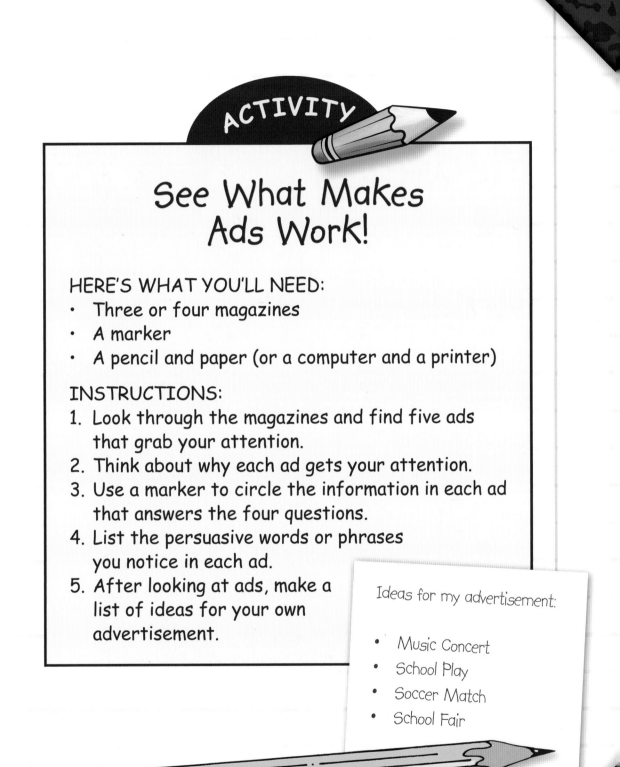

ACTIVITY

See What Makes Ads Work!

HERE'S WHAT YOU'LL NEED:
- Three or four magazines
- A marker
- A pencil and paper (or a computer and a printer)

INSTRUCTIONS:
1. Look through the magazines and find five ads that grab your attention.
2. Think about why each ad gets your attention.
3. Use a marker to circle the information in each ad that answers the four questions.
4. List the persuasive words or phrases you notice in each ad.
5. After looking at ads, make a list of ideas for your own advertisement.

Ideas for my advertisement:

- Music Concert
- School Play
- Soccer Match
- School Fair

CHAPTER THREE

Your Attention Please!

Before you write an ad, you need to know your **audience**. What group of people are you trying to reach? Use words that will appeal to that audience. It is a good idea to keep your sentences short. This will help your audience read your ad more quickly.

Imagine your school is having a fair to raise money for a new playground. You want as many students as possible to come to the fair. What could you say in an ad that would get the attention of other students? How could you persuade them to come?

Write for Your Audience!

HERE'S WHAT YOU'LL NEED:
- A pencil and paper (or a computer and a printer)

INSTRUCTIONS:
1. List the purpose of your ad.
2. Name the audience you hope to reach with your ad.
3. Which questions will your ad answer for the audience?
4. List words and phrases that will get your audience's attention and persuade them to do something.
5. Write the first **draft** of your ad. Remember to keep your sentences short!

Sample Ad Outline

PURPOSE OF YOUR AD:
To persuade students to come to the school fair

YOUR AUDIENCE:
Students at your school

QUESTIONS YOUR AD WILL ANSWER:
- What is happening? The Hillsdale School Fair
- Why should someone go to this event? To help raise money for a new school playground
- Where is this event happening? The Hillsdale School Gym
- When is this event happening? Saturday, April 13, from 8:00 a.m. to 1:00 p.m.

WORDS AND PHRASES THAT ARE PERSUASIVE AND GET ATTENTION:
- "Support our school!"
- "Help our school!"
- "Share in the excitement!"
- "Be with friends!"
- "Enjoy the action!"
- "Don't miss out on fun and games!"
- "Raise money for our school!"

HELP!

Sample First Draft of an Ad

Share in the excitement! Help our school!

The Hillsdale School Fair is Saturday, April 13!

The fair will be held in the Hillsdale School Gym
from 8:00 a.m. to 1:00 p.m.

Don't miss out on all the fun and games!

Tickets are only $10!

All money raised will be used
to build a new school playground.

CHAPTER FOUR

Made You Look!

Now you have decided which words to use in your ad! You also need to choose a **design** that will make your ad persuasive. Your audience will see the design first. Then they will read the words.

Bold letters and bright colors get people's attention. Picking the right picture to appear on the ad is another important step. Choose the design carefully. Don't try to fit too many words and pictures into your ad. Try different styles until you figure out which one works best!

Careful planning will pay off when it comes time to write your ad.

Decide on Your Design!

HERE'S WHAT YOU'LL NEED:
- Crayons or markers
- Paper

INSTRUCTIONS:
1. Try writing the words in different ways.
2. Try placing the words in different places on the paper.
3. Try different sizes and colors for the letters.
4. Try different pictures to go with your ad.
5. Make a **sketch** of the final ad.

CHAPTER FIVE

Bringing Everything Together

You are ready to do the final draft of your ad! Gather any materials you will need to do printing and create artwork. Have your first draft and your sketch handy. It is time to bring the words and the design together to share with your audience!

Your rough draft will help you create a better final ad.

17

Do the Final Draft!

HERE'S WHAT YOU'LL NEED:
- A copy of the first draft of your ad
- A copy of your design sketch
- Poster board or paper
- Crayons or markers
- Glue (if you are pasting pictures onto your ad)

INSTRUCTIONS:
1. Copy the words that will appear in your ad onto poster board or a new piece of paper.
2. Glue or redraw your pictures on the poster board or paper.
3. Admire your ad!

Share in the EXCITEMENT!
Help our school!

The Hillsdale School Fair is
Saturday, April 13
The fair will be held in the
Hillsdale School Gym
from 8:00 a.m. to 1:00 p.m.

Don't miss out on all the
FUN AND GAMES

TICKETS ARE ONLY $10

All money raised will be used to build a new school
PLAYGROUND

CHAPTER SIX

Final Check

STOP! DON'T WRITE IN THE BOOK!

ACTIVITY

Check Your Ad One More Time!

Ask yourself these questions as you reread your ad:

☐ YES ☐ NO Do I grab people's attention? (Ask a friend or family member if you are unsure!)

☐ YES ☐ NO Do I appeal to my audience?

☐ YES ☐ NO Do I give my audience all the information they need? (Think about whether you answer the four questions that ask what, why, where, and when.)

☐ YES ☐ NO Do I use persuasive words and phrases?

☐ YES ☐ NO Do I keep my sentences short?

☐ YES ☐ NO Do I use letters that are big and easy to read?

What should you do after you carefully check the final draft of your ad? Ask a teacher or parent if you should make copies. Discuss the best spots to place your ad. Pick areas where your audience is sure to see it. Does your school have a Web site? Ask your teacher if you can post your ad online.

What other ideas do you have for ads? Keep reading other people's ads and writing your own. Who knows? Someday you may get a job writing ads!

One day your ads could be on display for millions of people to see!

Glossary

advertisements (ad-vur-TIZ-muhntz) public notices used to sell a product or make an announcement

announcements (uh-NAUNT-smuhnts) written or spoken messages that tell people about an event

appeal (uh-PEEL) to cause people to like someone or something

attention (uh-TEN-shuhn) the act of looking at or listening to something closely and carefully

audience (AW-dee-uhntz) a group of people who view an ad

design (di-ZYNE) a plan for creating artwork and decorations

draft (DRAFT) an early version of a writing project

persuasive (pur-SWAY-siv) able to make people act or feel a certain way

sketch (SKECH) to make a rough drawing

For More Information

BOOKS

Boucher, Francoize. *I Love Words*. Tulsa, OK: Kane/Miller, A Division of EDC Publishing, 2010.

Connolly, Sean. *Advertisements*. Mankato, MN: Smart Apple Media, 2010.

WEB SITES

Federal Trade Commission (FTC)—Admongo
www.admongo.gov/
This site features sample ads and games that teach lessons about advertising.

PBS Kids Go!—Create Your Own Ad
www.pbskids.org/dontbuyit/advertisingtricks/
createyourownad_flash.html
Visit this Web site to practice creating an ad for soda.

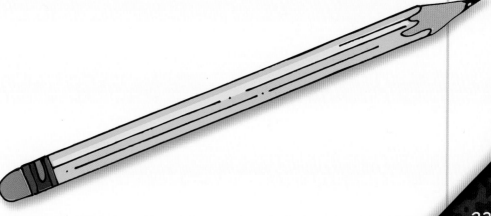

Index

action words, 8

announcements, 7

artwork, 15, 16, 17, 18

attention, 6, 9, 10, 11, 12, 15, 20

audiences, 10, 11, 14, 17, 20, 21

colors, 15, 16

copies, 21

designs, 14–15, 16, 17, 18, 20

event ads, 7, 10, 12

final draft, 17, 18–19, 21

first draft, 11, 13, 17, 18

information, 7–8, 9, 20

letters, 15, 16, 20

magazines, 6, 9

newspapers, 6

outlines, 11, 12

persuasion, 4, 5, 6, 8, 9, 10, 11, 12, 14, 20

phrases, 8, 9, 11, 12, 16, 20

placement, 21

printing, 17

questions, 7, 9, 11, 12, 20

sales ads, 6

sentences, 10, 11, 20

sketches, 16, 17, 18

words, 8, 9, 10, 11, 12, 14, 15, 16, 17, 18, 20

About the Authors

Cecilia Minden, PhD, is the former director of the Language and Literacy Program at Harvard Graduate School of Education. She earned her doctorate from the University of Virginia. While at Harvard, Dr. Minden also taught several writing courses. Her research focuses on early literacy skills and developing phonics curriculums. She is now a full-time literacy consultant and the author of more than 100 books for children. Dr. Minden lives with her family in Chapel Hill, North Carolina. She likes to write early in the morning while the house is still quiet.

Kate Roth has a doctorate from Harvard University in language and literacy and a master's degree from Columbia University Teachers College in curriculum and teaching. Her work focuses on writing instruction in the primary grades. She has taught kindergarten, first grade, and Reading Recovery. She has also instructed hundreds of teachers around the world in early-literacy practices. She lives in Shanghai, China, with her husband and three children, ages 2, 6, and 9. Together they do a lot of writing to stay in touch with friends and family and to record their experiences.